METROPOLITAN BOROUGH OF WIRRAL

Please return this book to the Library from which it was borrowed on or before the last date stamped. If not in demand books may be renewed by letter, telephone or in person. Fines will be charged on overdue books at the rate currently determined by the Borough Council.

012058		020817
030164	015019 015369	
	019507	
		018607
		133658

387.2

NORMAN, C.J.

Warships

S414450

METROPOLITAN BOROUGH OF WIRRAL SCHOOL LIBRARY SERVICE

DEPARTMENT OF LEISURE SERVICES + TOURISM LIBRARIES AND ARTS

PICTURE LIBRARY
WARSHIPS

PICTURE LIBRARY
WARSHIPS

C. J. Norman

Franklin Watts

London   New York   Sydney   Toronto

© 1986 Franklin Watts Ltd

First published in Great Britain
1986 by
Franklin Watts Ltd
12a Golden Square
London W1R 4BA

First published in the USA by
Franklin Watts Inc
387 Park Avenue South
New York
N.Y. 10016

First published in Australia by
Franklin Watts
14 Mars Road
Lane Cove
2066 NSW

UK ISBN: 0 86313 353 3
US ISBN: 0-531-10093-6
Library of Congress Catalog Card
Number: 85-51458

Printed in Italy
by Tipolitografia G. Canale & C. S.p.A. - Turin

Designed by
Barrett & Willard

Photographs by
N.S. Barrett Collection
British Aerospace
Fleet Photographic, Royal Navy
Ministry of Defence (UK)
Naval Photographic Center, Washington DC
Norwegian Embassy
Secretary of Defense, Pentagon

Illustrations by
Janos Marffy/Jillian Burgess Artists

Technical Consultant
Bernard Fitzsimons

Series Editor
N.S. Barrett

Contents

Introduction	6
The cruiser	8
Types of warships	10
Frigates and destroyers	12
Cruisers	18
Battleships	22
Other types of ships	24
The story of warships	28
Facts and records	30
Glossary	31
Index	32

Introduction

Warships play an important part in the defence of all the major nations. The oceans and seas make up more than two-thirds of the earth's surface, so warships cover vast areas.

The world's largest navies have several hundred warships. They operate in task forces of about ten ships.

△ An anti-aircraft destroyer of the Royal Navy. Destroyers are used to protect convoys against air attack.

Several kinds of warships make up a task force. These groups are usually centred around an aircraft carrier, which is often escorted on either side by anti-aircraft cruisers.

Other ships in a group include frigates, destroyers, hunter-killer submarines and various kinds of supply ships.

△ **USS** *Long Beach* is a very powerful cruiser. It is armed with missiles guided by radar.

The cruiser

The main picture shows a guided-missile cruiser. The smaller diagrams show the shapes and relative sizes of various warships.

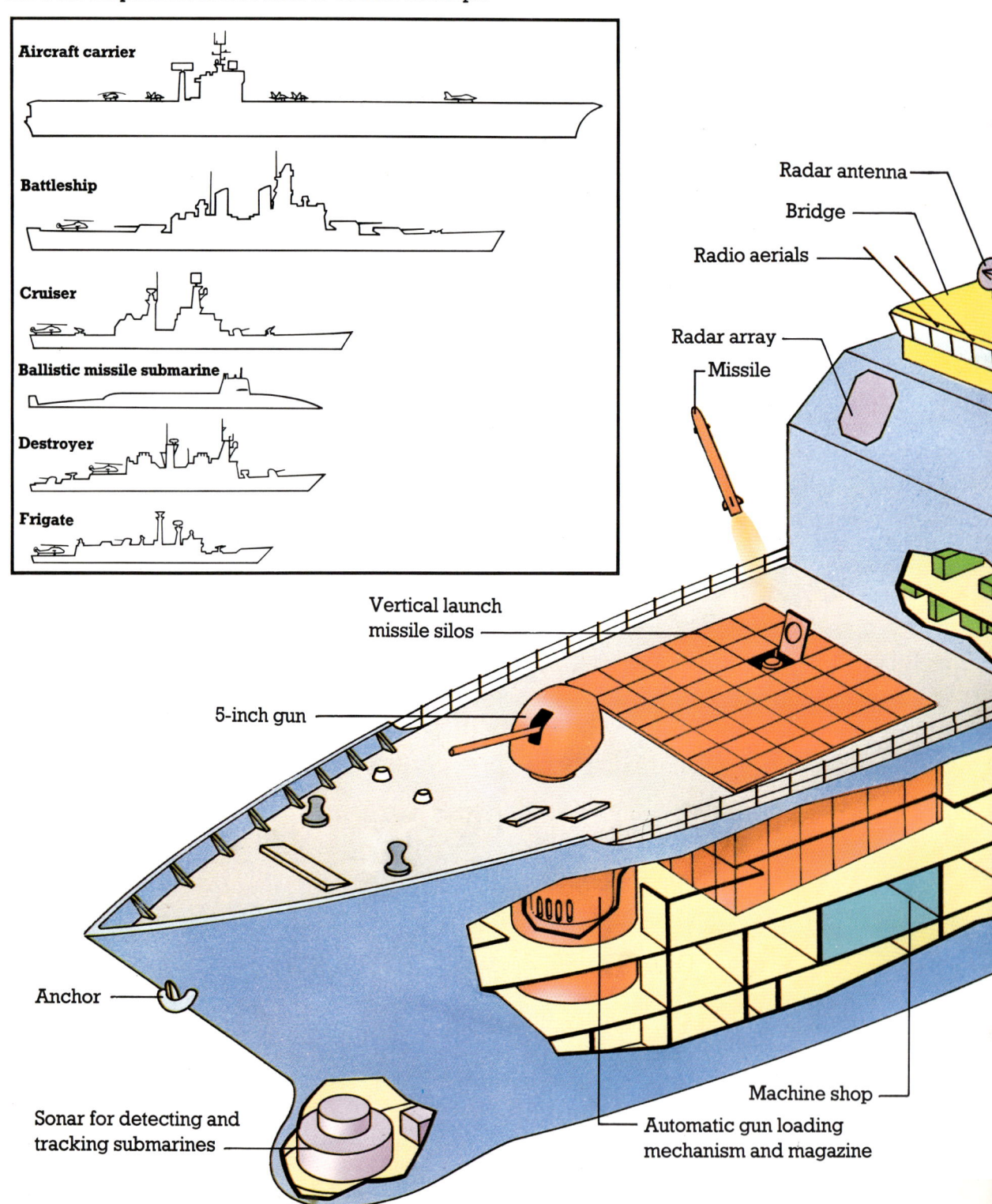

Aircraft carrier

Battleship

Cruiser

Ballistic missile submarine

Destroyer

Frigate

- Radar antenna
- Bridge
- Radio aerials
- Radar array
- Missile
- Vertical launch missile silos
- 5-inch gun
- Anchor
- Sonar for detecting and tracking submarines
- Machine shop
- Automatic gun loading mechanism and magazine

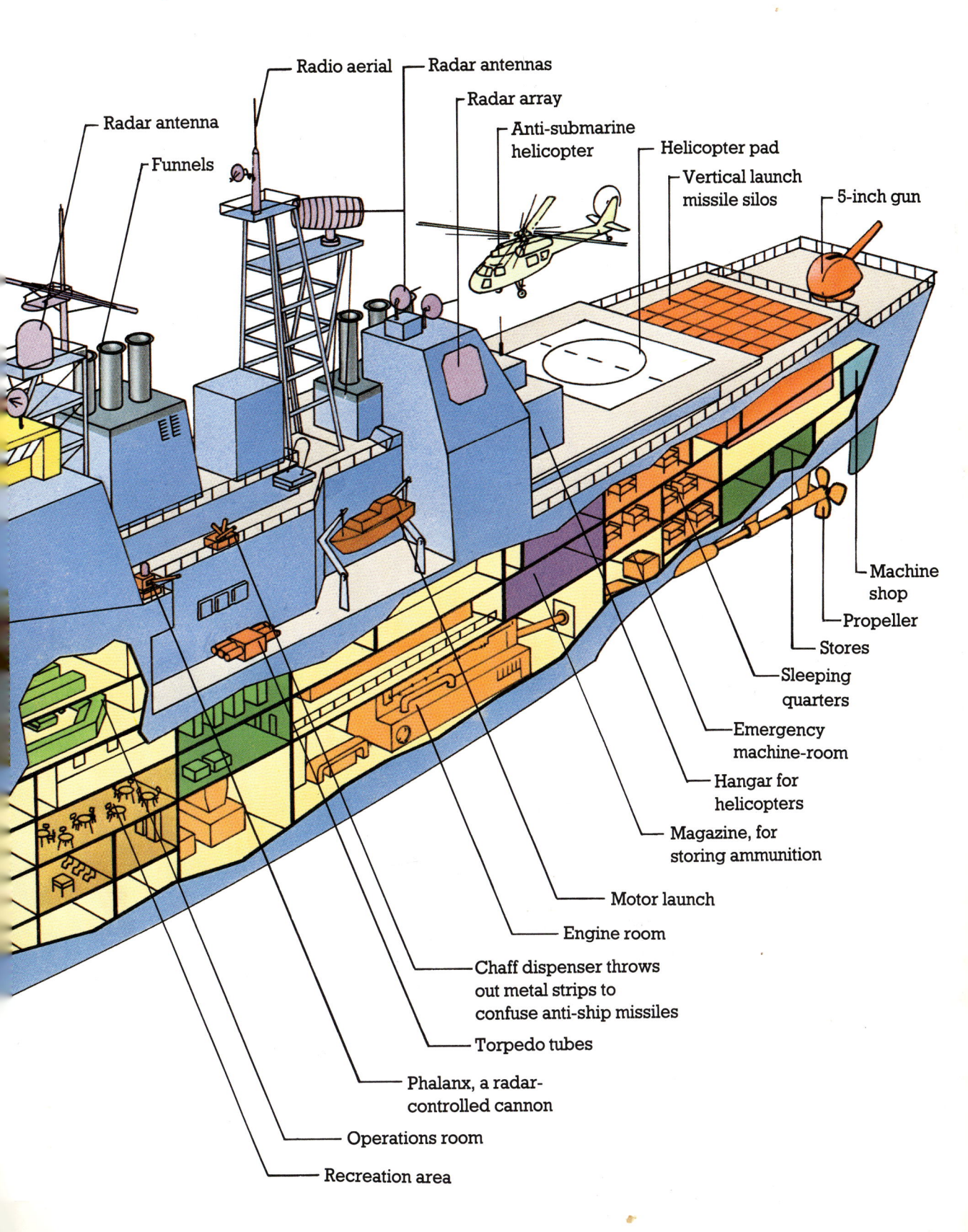

- Radar antenna
- Funnels
- Radio aerial
- Radar antennas
- Radar array
- Anti-submarine helicopter
- Helicopter pad
- Vertical launch missile silos
- 5-inch gun
- Machine shop
- Propeller
- Stores
- Sleeping quarters
- Emergency machine-room
- Hangar for helicopters
- Magazine, for storing ammunition
- Motor launch
- Engine room
- Chaff dispenser throws out metal strips to confuse anti-ship missiles
- Torpedo tubes
- Phalanx, a radar-controlled cannon
- Operations room
- Recreation area

9

Types of warships

The largest warships are the big US aircraft carriers. Next come the battleships, of which there are very few in operation, and then the cruisers. Destroyers and frigates form the bulk of warships in fleets. Some submarines operate alone.

Ships that work in coastal waters include missile craft, mine hunters and layers, patrol submarines and fast patrol boats.

▽ A show of strength from the US Navy. There are three aircraft carriers in this group, along with cruisers, destroyers, frigates and a tanker.

△ Missile boats of the Swedish Navy. These craft are armed with long-range guided missiles.

Frigates and destroyers

Frigates and destroyers are mostly escort vessels. Their chief role is to protect aircraft carriers or convoys of supply ships from enemy aircraft and submarines. Frigates are used chiefly to hunt and destroy submarines.

Destroyers are also used for other missions. They carry out search and rescue work at sea and they take part in the bombardment of enemy shores.

△ USS *John Young*, a Spruance-class destroyer. At nearly 8,000 tonnes, these are among the biggest destroyers afloat. They have a crew of nearly 300.

▷ Two frigates of the Royal Navy. The *Arrow* (top) is a Type 21 of 3,250 tonnes and 175 crew. It uses a Lynx helicopter for anti-submarine warfare. The *Broadsword* (below) is a Type 22 (4,200 tonnes) and has a crew of 224.

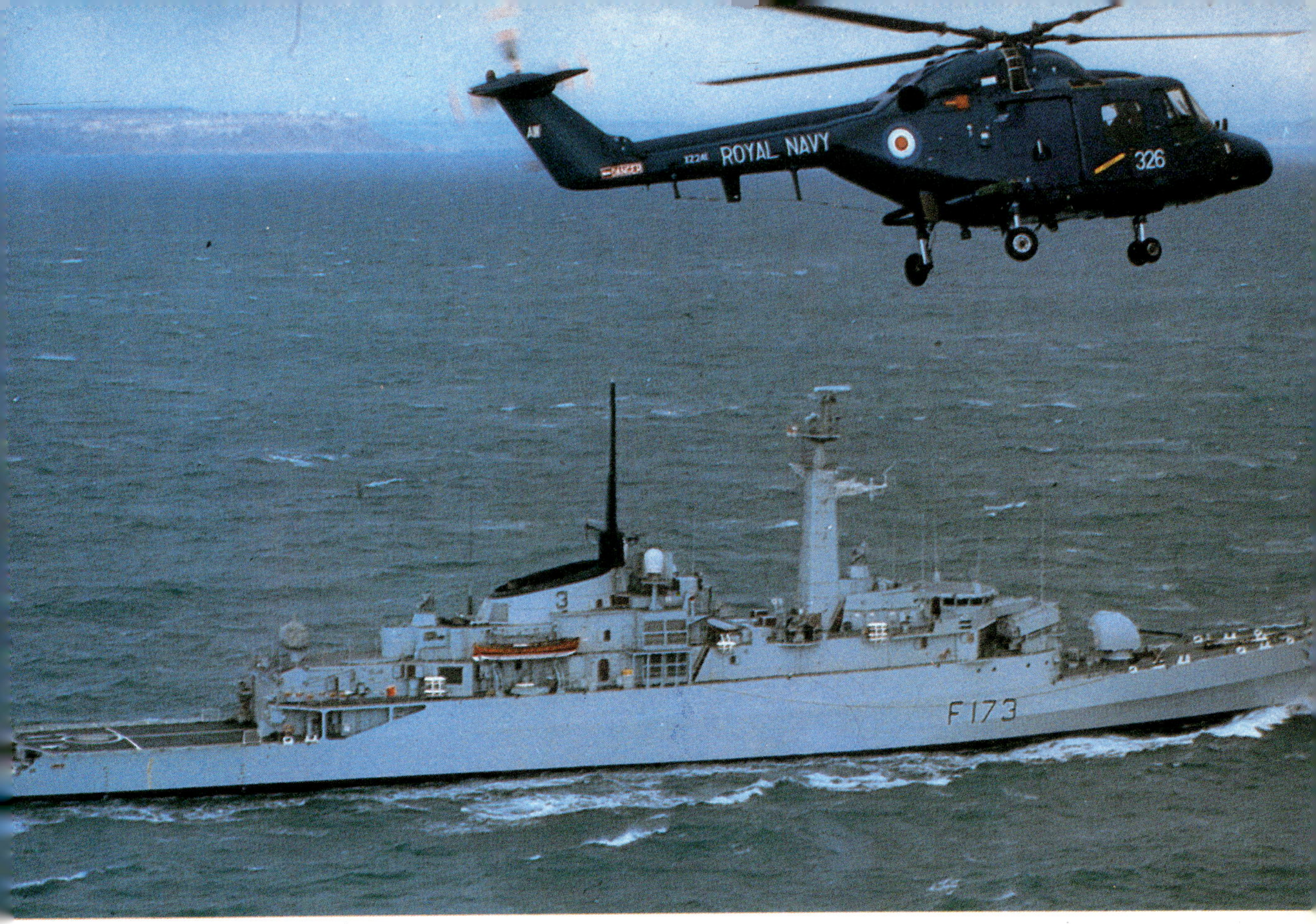
ROYAL NAVY
326
F173

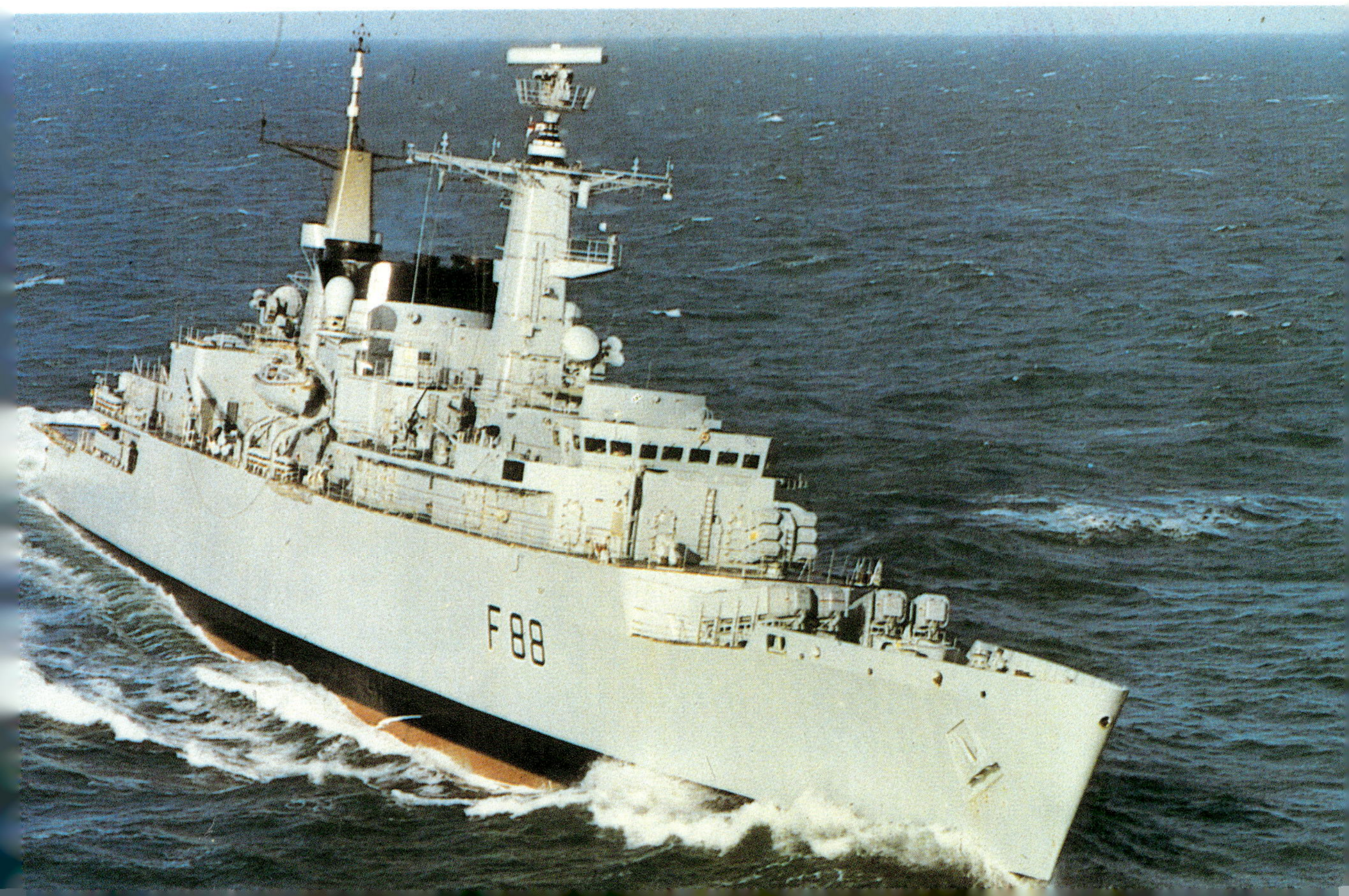
F88

▷ A Harpoon missile is fired from a destroyer, leaving a trail of smoke behind it. This is a long-range anti-ship missile. It is guided towards its target by its own computer, using information provided by the ship's radar. When the missile nears its target, it uses the same radar to home in on it.

The smaller picture shows a Tomahawk being launched. This is a long-range missile that can be used for targets at sea and on land. It can also be fitted with a nuclear warhead.

Missiles such as these give modern destroyers great fire power.

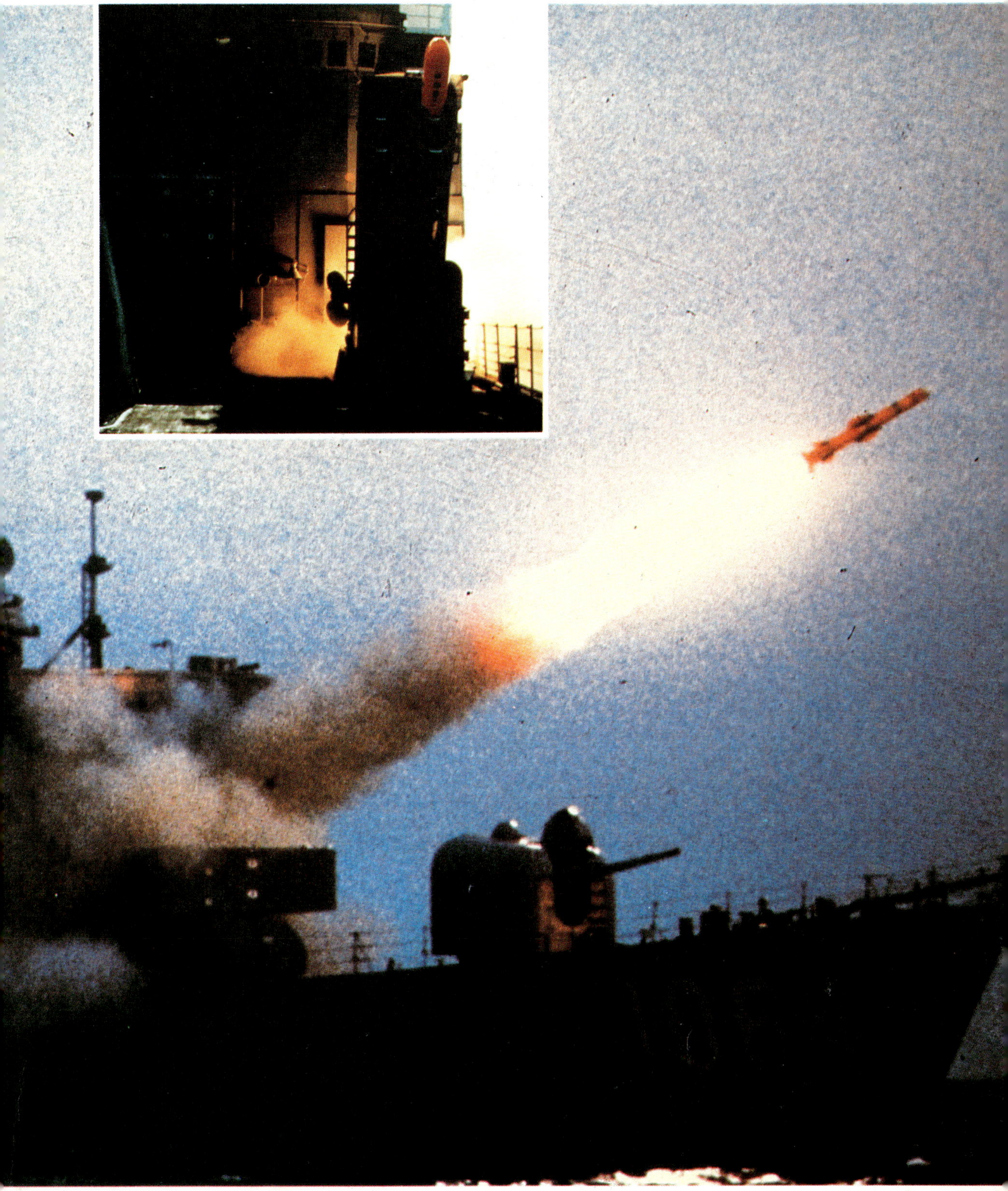

Frigates and destroyers are equipped with a wide range of weapons. They carry helicopters for detecting and attacking submarines.

Destroyers have anti-aircraft guns and anti-submarine weapons. They also have missiles for use against aircraft and other ships.

Frigates are equipped with anti-submarine weapons such as torpedoes and depth-charges. They use missiles to counter air and surface attack.

△ Short-range weapons that can be used against incoming missiles and attacking aircraft. The Seawolf (above) is being fired from a six-cell missile launcher. The Phalanx (left) is a rotary cannon. The large white radar dome tracks the target and fires automatically.

▷ The main mast of a destroyer is equipped with a mass of sensitive tracking equipment. The mast to the left belongs to a neighbouring cruiser.

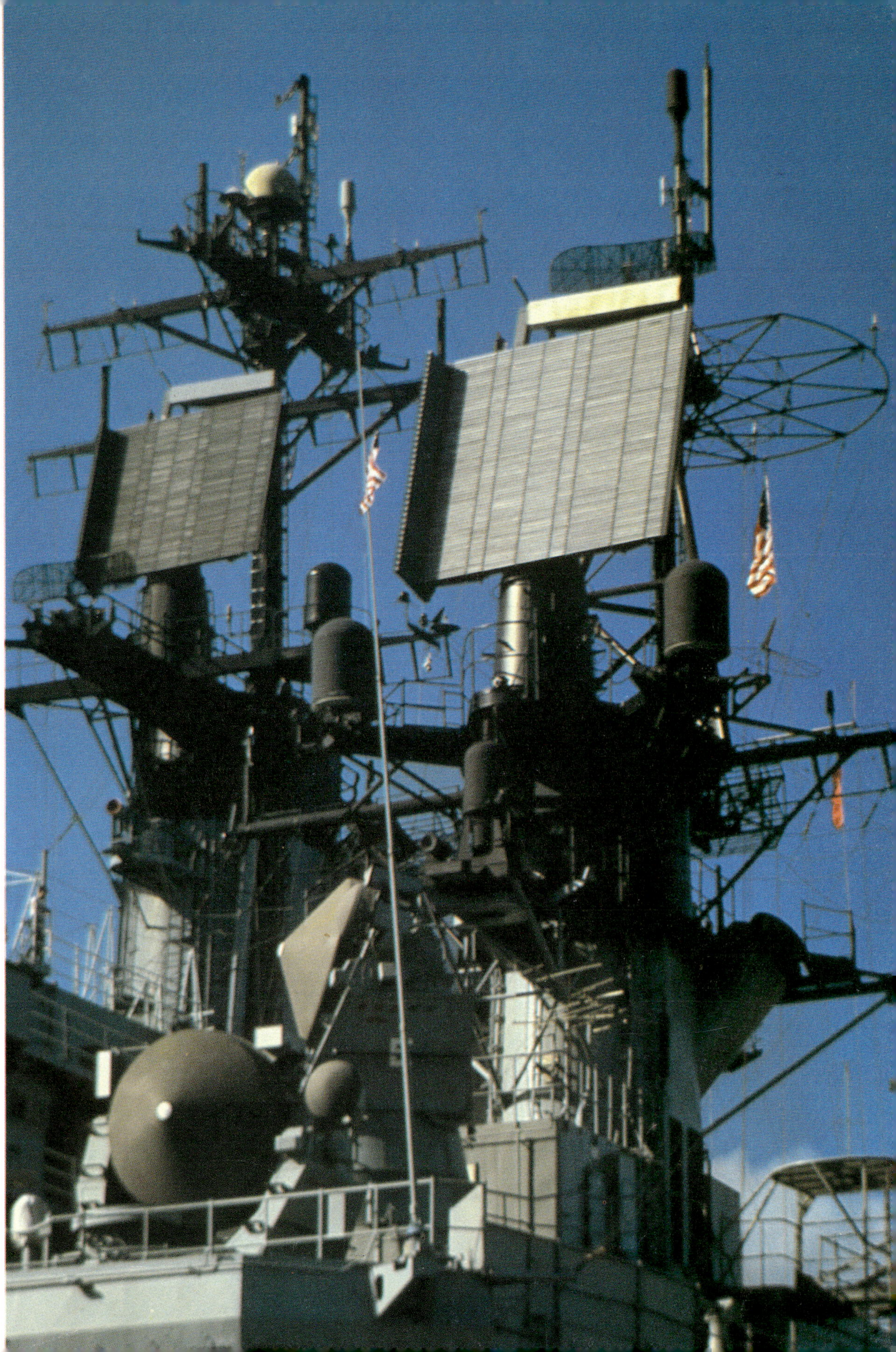

Cruisers

The US Navy has more than 30 cruisers, which are the largest of the escort vessels. Their chief role is to provide protection for the task group's aircraft carrier.

The Soviet Navy has more than 40 cruisers. It has few larger ships, so cruisers provide most of its sea power. Other navies have about a dozen cruisers between them.

△ **USS** *Ticonderoga* is a guided-missile cruiser of 9,600 tonnes. It has a crew of 375. The large structure at the front is the main surveillance radar. Unlike other radar, it does not revolve. Instead of scanning mechanically, it sends out electronic signals over a wide arc.

△ The *Marshal Timoshenko*, a Soviet cruiser of the Kresta II class. Soviet cruisers are very heavily armed with guns, missiles and other weapons.

◁ A front (far left) and a rear (left) view of *Mississippi*, a US guided-missile cruiser. It is used as an escort ship for aircraft carriers, and is nuclear powered to give it an unlimited range of operation.

19

Some cruisers run on nuclear power. This enables them to stay with their aircraft carrier on long missions without the need to be refuelled.

Cruisers are heavily armed. They are equipped with missiles, guns, torpedoes and depth-charges for use against enemy aircraft and submarines. Most cruisers carry two anti-submarine helicopters.

△ *Bainbridge*, a US cruiser, was launched in 1961. It is still in service, but needs a larger crew – nearly 550 – than modern cruisers.

▷ The launch of a Standard, a medium- to long-range missile. Standards are guided by radar and are used for air defence.

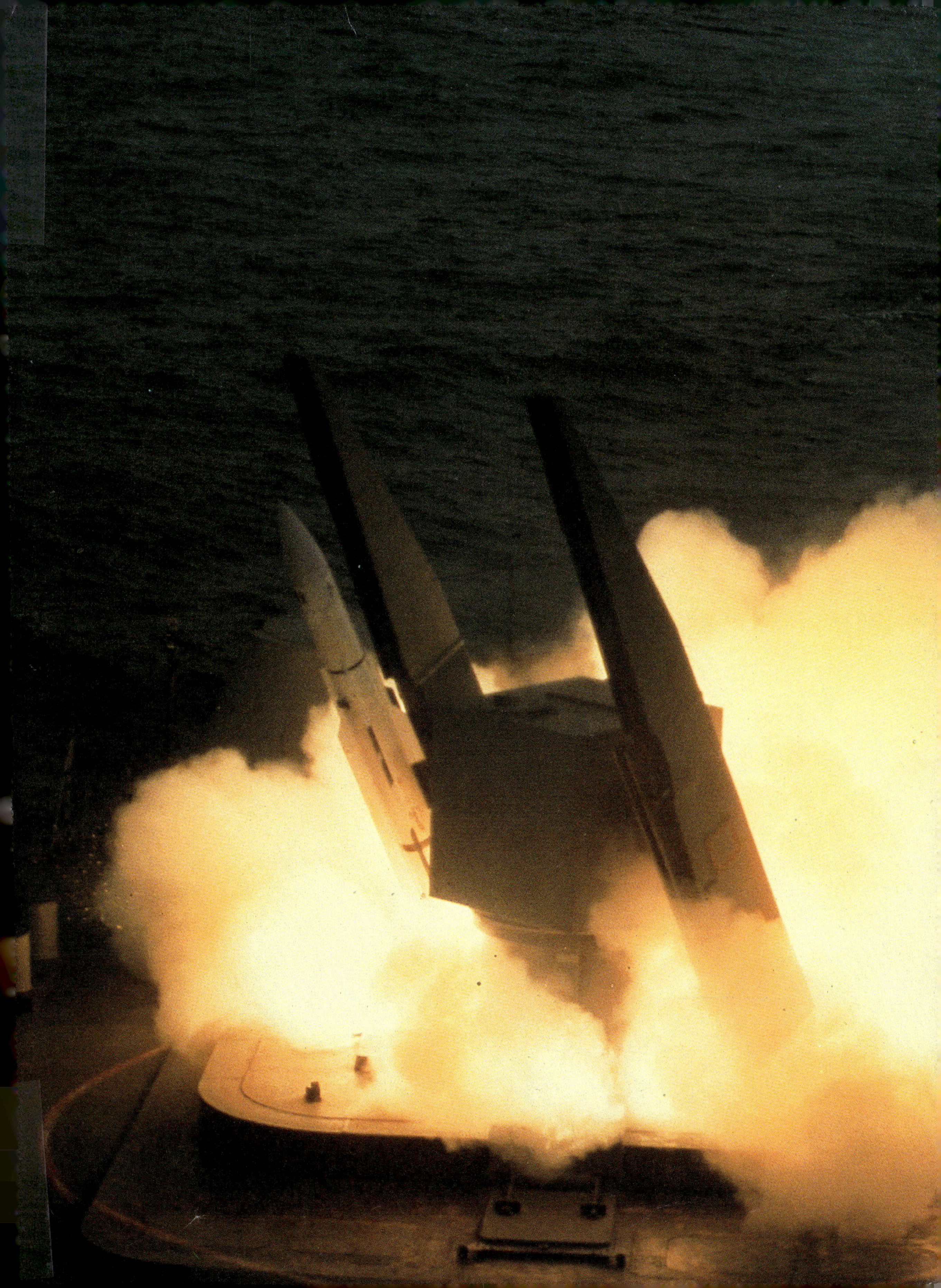

Battleships

Battleships were once the most powerful vessels in the world's navies. This role has now been taken over by aircraft carriers, which use planes and helicopters as their attacking force.

The US Navy has now begun to rebuild some of its old battleships. The Soviet Navy has begun to build battle-cruisers, which are not as large as battleships.

△ USS *New Jersey*, the first of the Iowa class battleships to be rebuilt and modernized in the 1980s. At 58,000 tonnes, *New Jersey* is bigger than all but the large US aircraft carriers. It has a crew of about 1,600.

▷ *New Jersey* with guns blazing, and (small picture) the massive 16 inch (406 mm) guns.

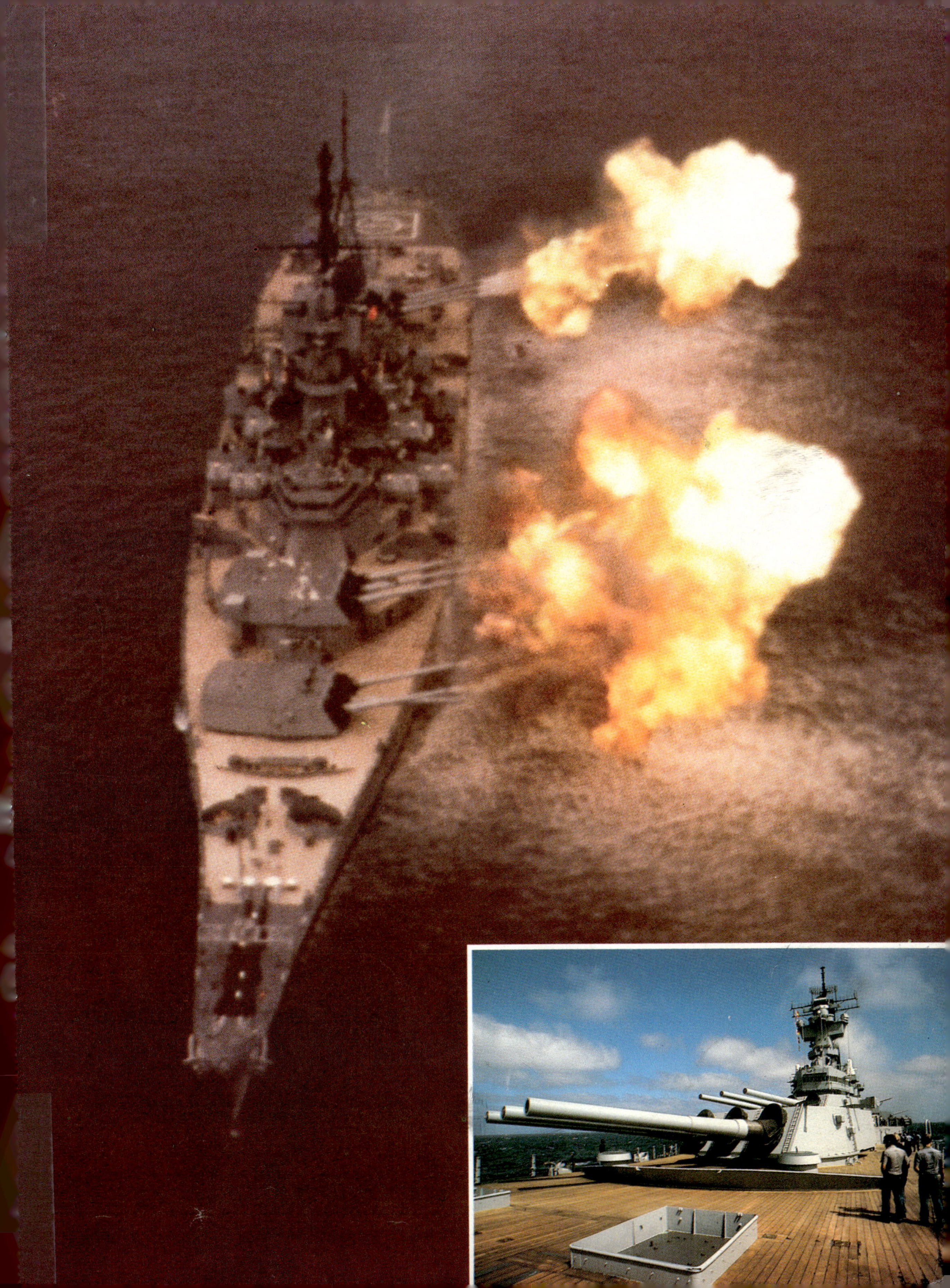

Other types of ships

Aircraft carriers and submarines dominate the world's oceans. The nuclear-powered vessels can go for years without refuelling.

Carriers are like floating airfields, with up to 100 aircraft operating from the larger ones. Ballistic-missile submarines are the deadliest warships of all. They carry long-range missiles capable of destroying cities.

△ The US carrier *Enterprise* is one of the biggest warships afloat. It has the distinction of being the longest – 342 m (1,123 ft). The large US carriers have a crew of five to six thousand.

Assault ships are used for landing marines and their supplies and equipment. Supply ships carry fuel and equipment for fighting vessels.

Ships that operate mainly in coastal waters include diesel submarines and small frigates called corvettes. Fast patrol boats attack shipping, mainly with missiles. Other important small craft are minelayers and minesweepers.

△ **USS** *Michigan* **is a ballistic-missile submarine. These nuclear-powered vessels carry 24 Trident inter-continental missiles, which they can launch from under the sea.**

△ The minesweeper HMS *Kirkliston*. Mine hunters operate in teams.

◁ HMS *Black Rover* is a fleet tanker. It carries fuel and other supplies for warships at sea.

▷ HMS *Fearless* (top) is an assault ship. The *Storm* (bottom) is a Norwegian missile boat.

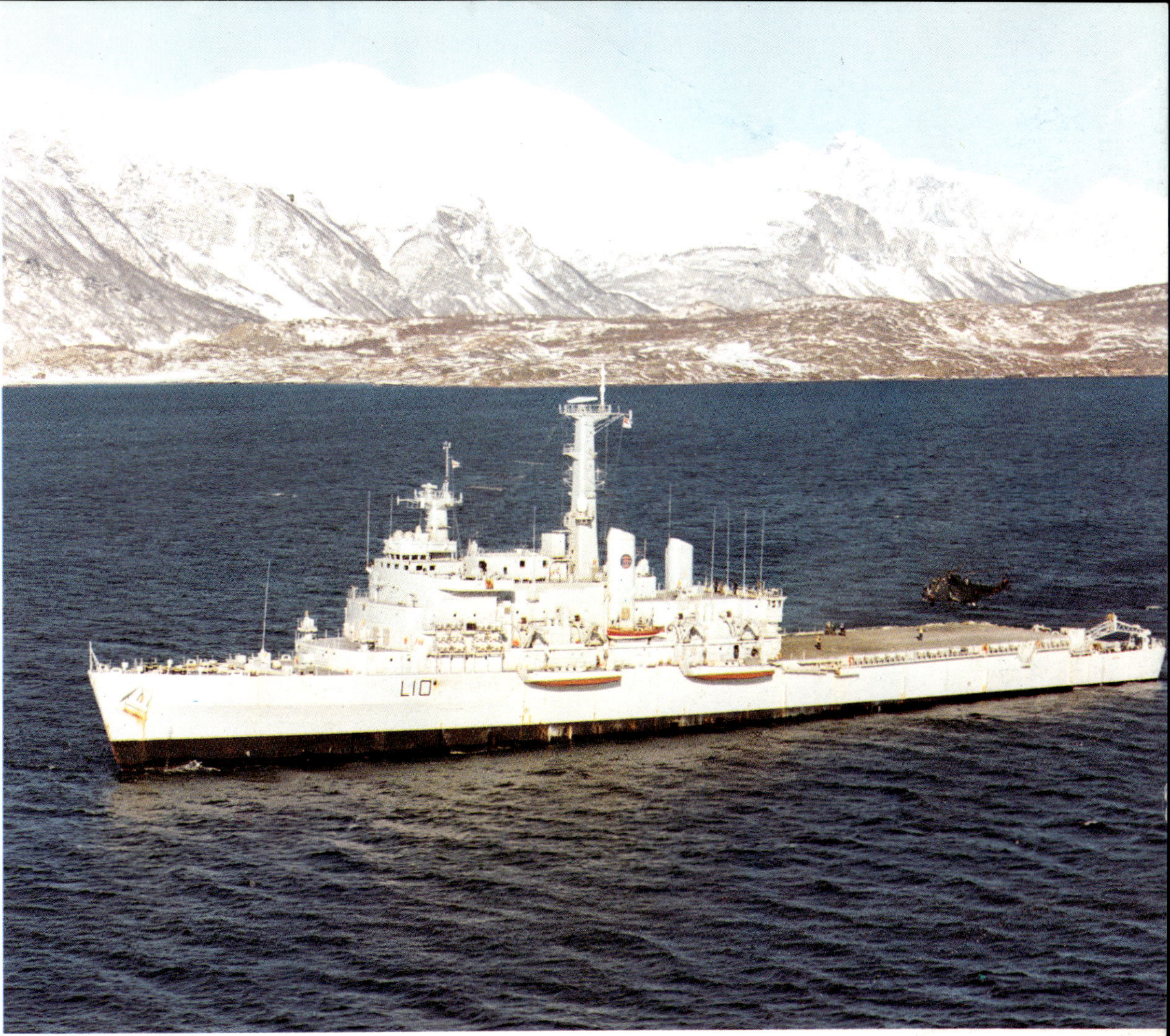

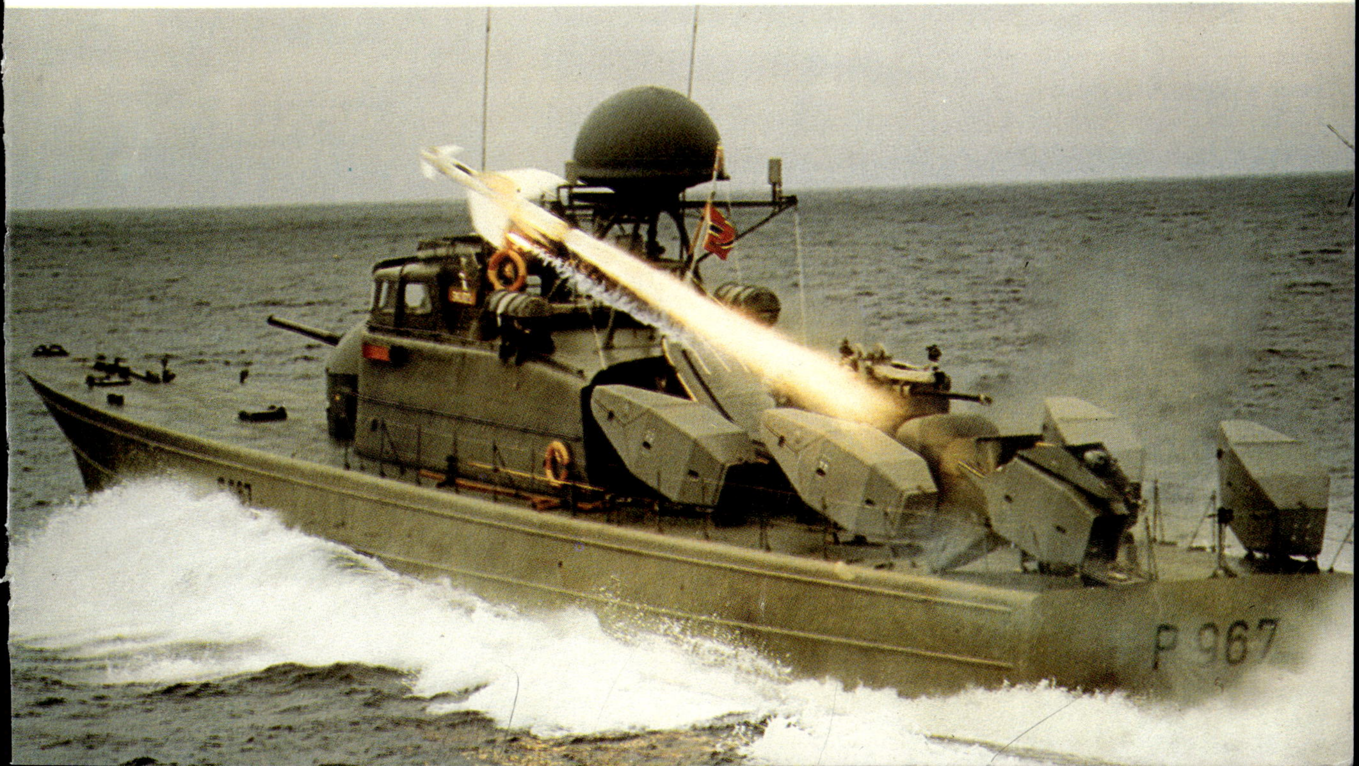

The story of warships

Fighting ships
Ships have been used for fighting for thousands of years. The ancient Greek and Roman navies used galleys, and about 1,000 years ago the Vikings of northern Europe ruled the seas with their longboats. All these ships were propelled by oarsmen, sometimes with the help of sails.

△ The galleon *Great Harry* (1514) was the first English battleship.

Galleons
In early sea battles, ships would ram each other. Fighting took place on the decks as crews tried to board other ships. By the 1500s, however, most ships carried guns. Navies began to build large sailing ships called galleons. These could be heavily armed for duty as warships. But many of them were difficult to manoeuvre in battle, as they were not designed for fighting.

Ships of the line
The great sailing warships of the 1600s to the early 1800s were called ships of the line. This was because they served in the line of battle. They were fast and manoeuvrable, and could carry more than 100 heavy guns.

△ Ships of the line taking part in the Battle of Trafalgar in 1805.

Steam and steel

△ A battle of steamships during the American Civil War. The Confederate cruiser *Alabama* was sunk in the English Channel by the US sloop-of-war *Kearsage* after destroying 68 ships in two years.

During the 1800s, steam-powered warships began to take over from sailing ships.

Another important development of the period was the use of explosive shells instead of solid cannonballs. For this reason, navies began to build ships of iron and then steel, instead of wood. Ships made of wood covered with iron were called ironclads.

The great battleships

The first modern battleship was the *Dreadnought*, introduced by the Royal Navy in 1906. All the major sea powers began to build these great battleships and they dominated the world's oceans until the early 1940s.

△ HMS *Dreadnought*, the first of the great 20th-century battleships.

Submarines and carriers

Submarines became the most feared warships in World War I (1914–18), and continued to

△ USS *New Jersey*, a battleship of the 1940s, was modernized in the 1980s.

destroy large and small ships in World War II (1939–45).

At the same time, with the development of warplanes, battleships were becoming less important. The aircraft carrier began to dominate the seas.

The nuclear age

Ships powered by nuclear fuel can sail the seas for years without the need to refuel. The biggest submarines and aircraft carriers are now nuclear powered.

△ The US carrier *Nimitz*, at 95,000 tonnes the largest warship afloat.

Facts and records

Clash of ironclads
One of the most famous sea fights in naval history was the clash between two ironclad ships in 1862 during the American Civil War. The *Merrimac*, an old wooden frigate abandoned by Federal forces, was rebuilt by the Confederates. Batteries of powerful guns were set up on deck and housed in heavy armour. The *Merrimac* went out and sank two enemy ships, as cannonballs bounced off it. The Union quickly brought the ironclad *Monitor* in to defend their fleet, and the two ships engaged in a long battle. Neither ship could penetrate the armour of the other in this first encounter between two ironclads. From that day it became obvious that greater fire power was needed.

△ The engagement between ironclads *Merrimac* (left) and *Monitor*.

The greatest battle
The greatest sea battle took place in the Pacific in 1944 during World War II, with 282 warships involved. Two great US fleets, with 216 warships, joined by 2 Australian ships, crushed the Japanese fleet of 64 ships in the Battle of Leyte Gulf.

Glossary

Assault ships
Vessels that carry helicopters, amphibious landing craft and marines for shore landings.

Ballistic missile submarine
A submarine armed with very long-range nuclear missiles that can be launched under water.

Battle-cruiser
A ship in between a battleship and a cruiser in size. It is lighter than a battleship and not as heavily armoured, but it is faster. It carries much more fire power than a cruiser.

Convoy
A group of supply ships escorted by armed warships.

Corvette
A small general-purpose vessel often used for escort or patrol duties.

Depth-charge
An anti-submarine bomb that is dropped from ships or aircraft and explodes under water.

Diesel submarine
A submarine that runs on diesel fuel and electric motors. It is also called a patrol submarine.

Escort vessel
An armed warship that accompanies an aircraft carrier or a group of merchant ships to protect them.

Fleet
A country's navy or a division of a navy under an admiral.

Hunter-killer submarine
A nuclear submarine that hunts and attacks enemy shipping as well as protecting its own ships.

Minesweepers
Vessels used for detecting and detonating mines. They are also called mine hunters.

Nuclear power
Power generated by a nuclear reactor. Reactors last for years without having their fuel replaced.

Supply ships
Vessels that carry fuel, ammunition, refrigerated stores or other supplies for warships at sea.

Task force
A group or a small fleet of ships, sometimes used for carrying out special missions.

Index

aircraft carrier 7, 8, 10, 12, 18, 19, 22, 24, 29
assault ship 25, 26, 31

Bainbridge 20
ballistic-missile submarine 8, 24, 25, 31
battle-cruiser 22, 31
battleship 8, 10, 22, 23, 28, 29
bridge 8

chaff dispenser 9
convoy 6, 12, 31
corvette 25, 31
cruiser 7, 8, 10, 17, 18, 19, 20, 21

depth-charge 16, 20, 31
destroyer 6, 7, 8, 10, 12, 13, 14, 16, 17
diesel submarine 25, 31
Dreadnought 28, 29

Enterprise 24
escort vessel 12, 18, 19, 31

fleet 10, 30, 31
frigate 7, 8, 10, 12, 13, 16, 25, 30

galleon 28
galley 28
guided-missile cruiser 19

Harpoon missile 14
helicopter 9, 13, 16, 20, 22
hunter-killer submarine 7, 31

John Young 12

Long Beach 7
longboat 28

Michigan 25
mine hunter 10, 26
minelayer 10, 25
minesweeper 25, 26, 31
missile 7, 8, 9, 10, 14, 16, 24, 25
missile craft 10, 11
Mississippi 19

New Jersey 22, 23, 29
nuclear power 20, 24, 25, 29, 31

patrol boat 10, 25
patrol submarine 10
Phalanx cannon 9, 16

radar 7, 8, 9, 14, 16, 18, 20

Seawolf missile 16
ship of the line 28
Standard missile 21
steamship 28, 29
submarine 7, 8, 10, 12, 16, 24, 29
supply ship 7, 12, 25, 26, 31

tanker 10, 26
task force 6, 7, 31
Ticonderoga 18
Tomahawk missile 14
torpedo 9, 16, 20
Trident missile 25

32